hi! i'm ann
one girl's witness

ann kiemel

BAKER BOOK HOUSE
Grand Rapids, Michigan

previously published under the title:
World-changing Love

the chorus quoted on page 15 is from the song "something
beautiful," copyrighted, 1971, by william j. gaither, and is
used by his permission. all rights are reserved.

Copyright 1974 by Beacon Hill Press

Reprinted by Baker Book House with permission of
Beacon Hill Press ISBN: 0-8010-5346-3

printed in the
united states of america

hi, i'm ann.

i'm an ordinary girl in a
very big world.
i walk down the street
and nobody picks me out of the crowd.

i board a plane about every weekend

to fly somewhere in the country

to speak

and nobody notices me.

i sit in a restaurant and eat

and i'm not special.

i'm a young girl
with a simple, young heart
in the middle of a . . . very . . .
very . . . big . . . world.
but i'm going to change my world.
you watch!

you wait!
you'll see . . . because
i have a giant of a God inside me
and i'm not scared.

i'm not afraid of war.
     of prejudice . . .
          of being different.

i'm not even scared of
     my own insignificance
          in a . . . very . . .
               big world.

God and i, with love,
     will push through the barriers.
          will crush the obstacles.

God and i, with love,
will change our world because
i believe in the kind of Christ that
chose common men—fishermen—
probably men with dirt
under their fingernails . . .
and some teeth missing.
because they loved Him it was YES, LORD,
to everything He asked of them.
He used 12 common, ordinary men
to literally move the world.

and i am just an ordinary girl . . .
but God and i are going to—
you watch.

◄► just two months ago i was on
an airplane going to kansas city.
the oklahoma city hockey team was on
the plane . . . sitting all around me.
a very nice-looking businessman
sat next to me.
we didn't have anything to say.
inside i was speaking with God.
"he's in my world . . . and, well . . .
if there is something You could use me
to say to him
. . . i would like that."

so . . . just as the plane was
beginning to descend,
this businessman turned to me
and said, "i don't like landing
at the kansas city airport. i
always feel as if we're going to land
on the railroad tracks."

i said, "oh, really . . . you know, i
taught school here for two years but
i had kinda forgotten about
the airport."
he said, "i don't believe you . . ."

"pardon . . ."

"i don't believe you taught school.
you are entirely too young
to have ever taught school.
how old are you . . . 16?"
i said, "sir, i'm 26 years of age, and
what would you say
if i told you i was the dean of women
on a college campus?"

he
    just
        blew
            his
                mind.

he said, "look at me, young lady . . .
i've been a jury trial lawyer for
21 years . . .
and i'm on my way to fort leavenworth
to interview a federal
murder prisoner,
    . . . and i couldn't do your job."

but i looked him in the eye . . .
and said, "you see, sir,
i have a giant of a Lord inside of me
and He and i together, we can do it."

i said, "i just learned a new
little song. would you like me to
sing it for you?"

"right here on the plane?" he asked.
"well, i said, "i don't have a very
good voice . . . but i know if
you heard my song
you would like it."
he said, "do you know
the oklahoma city hockey team is . . . ?"
"i know, sir, but i just know that
if you heard my song it would . . .

"alright . . . if you can keep it down
kind of soft."

so i looked him in the eye . . .
and i began to sing the story
of my life.

        something beautiful,
           something good . . .
        all my confusion
           He understood.
        all i had to offer Him
           was brokenness and strife—
        but He made
           something beautiful
        . . . of my life.

        he said, "young lady,
        that was beautiful. what do you
        really do?"

and i looked him in the eye and said,
"you see, sir, i change my world."

just about then
the plane touched the runway
and he said, "it's noon.
do you have plans for lunch?"
i said, "well, sir,
some friends are meeting me
and i am sure they probably do."
he said, "if they are not there,
may i buy your lunch for you?
i want to talk with you more
about your God."

dr. and mrs. hugh c. benner were to
pick me up, and if you know them,
you know they are very prompt.
but i couldn't believe
when i got off the plane,
there was no one there to meet me.
over lunch i shared with
a jury trial lawyer of 21 years
my Christ.
how my Christ could make
a better man out of him,
a better father,
a better lawyer in his world.
he went to pay the bill
and then he came back to me.

he shook my hand,
looked me in the eye,
and said,
"ann, i think i have found
what i have been looking for
all these years."

i went outside and stood
in front of the kansas city airport
with the cold wind blowing in my face.
and i threw my head back
and laughed with a great Lord.
i really believe that i,
an ordinary girl
in a very big world,
had changed my world in a little way
because i reminded a jury trial lawyer
that a great Lord
lives and loves and will walk with him.

◄►i was on my way to the airport

with my family after a good rest

and i whispered,

"Jesus, would You set someone next to

me on the plane that

i could share with?

i feel so rested and

i would like to talk with someone."

we were in the PSA terminal
and my father had his arm around me.
we were laughing together
and suddenly a man, perhaps
in his sixties, walked up and said,
"excuse me, sir,
is this young lady your daughter?"
my father said, "yes, she is."
the man said, "i've been watching her
from over there in that chair.
there is something very intriguing
and different about her.

sir, could i have your permission
to sit next to her on the plane
going home?"

my father said, "well, yes,
i guess it would be alright."
but when he started to put me
on the plane he whispered,
"honey, now be careful;
you can never tell about these older
men, you know."

i boarded the plane and
he was seated there with an empty seat
next to him.

he reached out his hand and said,
"hello, young lady;
my name is dr. bill boddy.
i have a ph.d. in journalism
and i travel around the world
for UPI and associated press.
i interview the leaders of our world,
the people you read about
in the newspaper every day.
they are the people i live with,
and breathe with, and talk to.

but there is something different about
you. tell me. what is it?"

i looked dr. bill boddy in the eyes
and said, "hi, sir.
my name is ann.
do you really want to know?"

"that's why i asked," he said.
i said, "i'm so excited about
my Christ.

He loves me.

He loves me even when i fail.

He loves me when nobody else will.

He understands me.

He laughs with me and cries with me.

and, sir, my Christ and i
are out to change our world with love.
you watch."

he sat there shaking his head.
he said, "i'm sorry, ann;
i can't share your hope.
one month ago today
my 27-year-old surgeon son was
killed in vietnam
and i'm just returning with his body
to meet my wife."

i said, "sir,

may i tell you my story?

i'm a young girl in a very big world

but, as a little girl,

my father used to take me on walks

and tousle my hair and say,

'ann, above anything and everything

else that ever happens to you,

remember this,

it pays to serve Jesus,'"

i began to share with him my story—

the hard moments,

the laughter,

the hurts—but how Jesus

had really been my friend

and loved me,

and how it paid to serve Him.

tears ran down
this hard newsman's face.
he said, "stop."
he took off his glasses
and smeared the tears
and kinda sniffed and said,
"you're not lying to me, are you?"
"sir, i wouldn't lie to you."

"you're really telling me the truth?"

"i am, sir."

he shoved his glasses back on
and rubbed his nose.
"go on, tell me some more."
and i shared with him my Christ
as he wept.
it wasn't long until the businessmen
behind us were leaning over
and the ladies across the aisle
were leaning over.
i said, "boy, God, this
is pretty exciting!
i asked for one person and You
have given me nearly the whole plane."

as we started to land, he said,
"ann, my wife is waiting at the gate
and she is so broken up—
do you think you could share with her
the hope you shared with me?"

we went to a coffee shop
and with tears spilling down her face
and mine into our coffee
i shared with her a great Lord
who could walk with her.
i told her that Jesus Christ could
share her pain and hurt
and soothe her heart because
He loved her.
today dr. and mrs. bill boddy are
somewhere in the world
and he is interviewing important people;
but i really believe that i,
an ordinary young girl,
was able to change my world
in just a little way
because i reminded him and his wife
that a great Lord lived and loved
and would walk with them.

◄► i am going to change my world.

                         you watch.

    you'll see.

    because i have a giant of a Lord

                    inside of me,

    and He and i with love

    will push through the barriers.

                 i'm not afraid.

"by this shall all men know that
ye are my disciples,
if ye have love one to another."
not that you carry a big, fat Bible
under your arm
everywhere you go.
not that you slap each other
on the back and tell each other
what God can do
for your lousy tempers.
but,
"by this shall all men know that
ye are my disciples, if ye have love."

◄►when i went to long beach, calif.,

    i had 88 teen-agers and i told them that

    if we could just learn

    to love each other,

    God would trust us with the world.

    we began to learn to love each other.

    then God began to send a world in to us.

    we reached into the surrounding

    neighborhoods and started clubs.

    a year and a half later

    every week

    we had several hundred teen-agers

    in our ministry—

    not because of an outstanding program

    but simply because 88 teen-agers

    let a great Lord

    love through them.

        blessing.

            joy.

you see, you just can't stop love.

love never gives up.

love pushes through the barriers.

love always wins.

i need you to dream with me.
i need you to believe in a great Lord
with me.
i need you to love me in my world.
i need you to walk down the street
and reach out and say,
"hey, brother, may i take your hand
and walk with you?
and you, sister, and you?
may i laugh with you
and cry with you,
and may God and i share
your lonely roads with you?"
you and God
with love
can change **your** world, too.

◄►there was a little boy named chad.
　　he didn't make it very well
　　in the neighborhood because
　　he was shy
　　and didn't know how to make friends
　　very well. every afternoon
　　his mother watched the children coming
　　home from school.
　　there was always a big gang of kids,
　　but always chad walked behind
　　alone.

one day chad came in and said,
"you know what, mom?
valentine's day is coming up.
mom, do you think that i could make
valentines
for every kid in my class?"
inside, her heart just sank.
she knew that he would work so hard
and probably no one
would give him a valentine.
she didn't want him hurt.
but she looked down into
his eager little face and said,
"okay, darling, we will."

they bought rickrack and paints
and glue and paper.
for three weeks chad worked
to make 33 beautiful valentines.
then the big day came.
boy, was he excited!
he crammed the valentines under
his arms and in his hands and headed
out the door with his head high.
that afternoon the teacher said,
"alright, boys and girls,
everybody sit down.
i have a packet
for every boy and girl in the room.
you may bring your valentines
and put them in the packets."

chad gathered up his 33 valentines and
started putting them in the packets.
when all were through the teacher said,
"alright, boys and girls,
as i call your names,
you may come and get your packets.
you may open them
as soon as you get to your seats."

boy, was chad excited!

she began to call out names
and pass out packets.
finally she called chad's name.
he jumped up
and ran to get his packet.
he ran back to his seat
and tore it open. there was

one
valentine
inside.

chad's mother was quite sure
this would be a hard day for him.
"i know—i'll make some homemade
cookies and have a glass of cold milk
waiting for him when he comes home,"
she said to herself. so that afternoon
she put a big plate of warm cookies
on the table, along with cold milk.
she went over to the window,
wiped away the frost,
and began to watch.
pretty soon the big gang of kids came
laughing, talking,
valentines tucked under their arms.
boy, were they excited!
just a little behind walked chad—
alone.

no friend with him.

one valentine in his hand.

but his mother noticed he was walking
a little faster than usual.

she thought, "i know, he is about to
burst into tears. i'll run and
open the door for him
before anybody sees him."
she ran, threw open the door, and said,
"hi, darling, mommie has warm cookies
and milk for you on the table."

he didn't even hear her.
he walked right by.
his face was almost glowing. then
he turned around and ran back to her.
he threw his arms around her neck,
squeezed her, and said "o mommie,
guess what!
i had 33 valentines and there were
33 kids
i had a valentine for every kid
in my class."
she could hardly believe her ears.
he hadn't noticed that others
had done him wrong.
he forgot that he had received
only one.

that kind of love—
the kind of love that says,
"hey, brother, may i walk with you
even if you don't care about me?"
the kind of love
a sunday school teacher shows
on the ordinary days
when nobody notices.
the kind of love that says,
"i will understand you,
i will accept you even when
you are weak."
the kind of love that says,
"i will forgive you if you fail me."
God and i and that kind of love
will move our world.

◄►how big is your God?

how strongly do you believe in love

to smooth the barriers in your world

today?

how much do you care about the

neighbor down the street?

it's like the little boy in the class

in a church where i spoke recently.

on a sunday morning

after the worship service

a lady came out saying,

"did you hear the kids screaming?"

i said, "no, i didn't.

was some child . . . ?"

"yeah," she said,

"this little kid is such a problem.

i can hardly take it.

he let out a bloodcurdling cry

and i thought everyone in the church

probably heard him."

i said, "do you love him?"

she said, "of course i love him.

i grabbed him by the arm,
yanked him back down in his chair,
and said, 'honey, i love you,
but i'm not going to let you do this.'"
i said, "tell me something, lady,
have you ever been to his house?
have you ever eaten
an ice-cream cone with him?
have you ever thrown a ball with him?
lady, he's not dumb.
you can't look a little boy in the eye
and tell him you love him
and not know anything about
his world."

God and i

with love

will change our world.

reuben welch taught me a little song

that goes, "alleluia, alleluia!"

you know what that means . . .

"praise the Lord!"

"Jesus, thank You that
i'm just an ordinary girl
but i can have hope in a big world.
Jesus, thank You that You can use me,
one young girl in a big world,
to move it.
Jesus, thank You that
there is hope in the middle of

   war

      and chaos

        and fear

          because You live."

do you feel hope?
do you feel like saying,
"thank You, Jesus, that
You and i, with love, can
crash through barriers.
we can reach out to the businessman
next to us, where we work.
we can love the children in our block.
mothers can reach out
to other mothers,
women can reach out to other women.
we can walk lonely roads with them.
we can laugh with them
and care for them"?
do you believe that way with me today?

◄► i was just boarding a 747 to fly
to hawaii. i noticed at the gate
a young GI and his wife
weeping.
i whispered,
"God, if You'll put him
right next to me on the plane,
i'll tell him about You."
so we boarded the plane.
most of you have probably been in
a 747—they're so big.
we were on the same row but
i was on the far seat on one side
of the plane and he was
on the other side on the other end.
I said, "well, God, You blew it.
You really blew it.

i'll never be able to touch him
clear over there.
if You had put him right next to me,
but, God¬"

the whole flight i kept looking over
at him. the stewardess would say,
"would you like your dinner?"
i would watch him get his hanky
and wipe his eyes
and stare out the window.
inside, my heart was pounding.
i said, "God—i mean,
there is no way in the world
i can get over to him and, anyway,
i'm just a young girl.
he would think i was flirting
or something."

and then i began to cry. i said,
"o Jesus, how can i tell people
across the country
that You and i and love
are going to change the world if
i don't have the courage to go over
to that man and tell him You care
and You feel with him?"
it was near the end of the flight
and my heart was pounding harder.
i bit my tongue, and then
the man next to him got up to return
a magazine. i didn't know how
i was going to do it.
here was this whole line of bodies
that i had to crawl over
to get to him.
but i got up and said,

"oh, excuse me, sir,
i didn't mean to step on you.
oh, forgive me, sir;
can i help you pick up those things?"
and i crawled on
stumbling over body after body until
i fell into the seat next to this man.
he turned and looked at me. i said,
"hi, sir; my name is ann and—
well, sir, i noticed you were crying
when you boarded the plane.
are you going somewhere far?"
"yeah."
"are you going to be gone
a long time?"
"yeah, a year."
"was that your wife?"
"yeah, we've been married
only two weeks."

"sir, i'm a Christian, and you see,
Jesus Christ is my Friend and Saviour.
i know what it is like to feel lonely.
i felt lonely a lot of times
in my life and, sir,
i just wanted to tell you God and i
will walk the lonely road with you
and i want you to know—"
and i reached out my hand.
"i'll walk the lonely road with you
and your wife too.
and pray for you."
he said, "i can't believe it.
are you telling me you crawled over
all those guys from clear over there
to tell me that?"
"i know it seems kind of foolish.
i didn't want to do anything
that would be overbearing but . . ."

tears began to run down his face.
he said. "nobody ever cared for me
like that before."
he reached out
and took hold of my hand and said,
"thank you very much.
you know, i really feel i can make it
now. i think i can go on—
God and me."
i said, "i'd better get back
to my seat."

somewhere

walked a young man with hope.

i knew i had changed my world in a

little way because

i had reminded him that a great Lord

lived

and loved

and would walk with him.

will you

help me spread that word

to our world?

can we sing "alleluia"?
    alleluia, alleluia,
    alleluia, alleluia,
    alleluia, alleluia,
    alleluia, alleluia!

thank You, Jesus, very much
for hope in our world
today.

thank You, Jesus,
that we don't have to be
defeated by obstacles.

thank You, Jesus, that we,
with Your love,
can push through every barrier
and crush every obstacle
and can really change our world.